# Pool  [5 choruses]

Endi Bogue Hartigan

# Pool  [5 choruses]

### Endi Bogue Hartigan

OMNIDAWN PUBLISHING
RICHMOND, CALIFORNIA
2014

Cover artwork: *Ascent*. Oil on canvas. Betty Merken, artist.
Courtesy of the artist and Laura Russo Gallery, Portland, Oregon.
For more information, see bettymerkenstudios.com or laurarusso.com
Author photo by Emerald Walker
Book cover and interior design by Peter Burghardt


*Balcón* (Balcony) from Lorca's *Poema del cante Jondo* by Federico García Lorca copyright
© Herederos de Federico García Lorca, from *Obras Completas* (Galaxia/Gutenberg, 1996
edition). Excerpts from English-language Translations by W.S. Merwin, copyright ©
W.S. Merwin and Herederos de Federico García Lorca, and by Carlos Bauer, copyright
© C. Bauer and Herederos de Federico García Lorca. All rights reserved. For information
regarding rights and permissions of Lorca's works in Spanish, English or any other
language, please contact lorca@artslaw.co.uk or William Peter Kosmas, Esq.,
8 Franklin Square, London W14 9UU, England.


Offset printed in the United States
by Edwards Brothers Malloy, Ann Arbor, Michigan
on 55# Enviro Natural, 100% Recycled, 100% PCW
Acid Free Archival Quality FSC Certified Paper
with Rainbow FSC Certified Colored End Papers


Library of Congress Cataloging-in-Publication Data

Hartigan, Endi Bogue.
[Poems. Selections]
Pool (5 choruses) / Endi Bogue Hartigan.
  pages cm
ISBN 978-1-890650-92-6 (Trade Paperback : acid-free paper)
I. Title.
PS3608.A78725A6 2014
811'.6--dc23
                                        2013045791


Published by Omnidawn Publishing, Richmond, California
www.omnidawn.com    (510) 237-5472    (800) 792-4957
        10  9  8  7  6  5  4  3  2  1
        ISBN: 978-1-890650-89-6

# Contents

*—to Patrick and Jackson*

"...That same Lola
who looked so long
at herself in the pool."

—*Balcón*, Federico García Lorca, translated by W.S. Merwin

"Physically, there is no difference between sound and noise. Sound is a sensory perception and the complex pattern of sound waves is labeled noise, music, speech etc. Noise is thus defined as unwanted sound."

—World Health Organization, *Guidelines for Community Noise*

*1. gallop*

*We cannot help ourselves*
*but believe. Look what people do.*
*We cannot help ourselves to*
*believe. Look what people do*

*and believe. I can't believe it*
*said the plum trees shivering*

*and then the blossoms showed*
*up scattered, sideblown,*
*not just down. We cannot help*
*ourselves to everything*

*said the people unbelieving,*
*shaking heads. How can we believe now, look?*

*Atrocities blossom also, look.*

*The trees said help yourselves*

*to blossoms: democratic trees,*
*dreaming lessons. We believe*
*in teaching belief said the trees.*

*We cannot help ourselves with*
*blossoms, to blossoms of belief.*

*White blossoms fell on our hair*
*a weight barely there, so we*

*left them till they blew.*

## *Slippage and red poppies*
—after *Field of Poppies*, Charles-François Daubigny, 1874


—

How many poppies? *10,000,000 poppies.* How many poppies? *Negative 10 poppies.*
How many poppies? *Hope in the shape of poppies.* How many poppies? *Estimated hope.*
Were you among the poppies? She was among imagined poppies.
She can't quite begin.


—

A woman is the black movement on a horse in the distance beyond the poppies.
She has to begin again at the slippage of red poppies.
We have to begin at the slippage of alertness into fear.

She has to begin again at the various horizontal lifts in the field demonstrated
by the heads of the poppies,

like the heads of a crowd.
She has to weed herself out again of the gallop into form, and then?
She can't quite begin.


—

How many poppies? *Flooded poppies.* How many poppies? *Inside-out poppies.*
She has to begin again by the trademarks of poppies and machine guns and ships:
however repeated however loud.

The crowd is in a rally for existence as one hoped to impress

by red poppies, something of concrete subsistence, a presidential rally
where the poppies are tallied and loud.

—

*A crowd today is what can happen to a crowd. A crowd today is what can happen in a crowd.*
Gunfire upon a crowd in Mumbai. The skin-thin petals of the poppies.
The proliferation of gunfire, the proliferation of redness and skin, and then?



—

We can barely see a woman as a black movement on a horse, beyond the poppies.
She is the black movement beyond
10,000 (*approximate*) poppies, or beyond the paint that blurs

and estimates a crowd. The paint says
multiplicity blanketing but she is singular in a black movement, riding back.



—

How many poppies? *10,000,000 poppies.* How many poppies? *Negative red poppies.*
What's the negative of red? Transparency surrounding poppies in which we stand
alert, alertness slipping into fear.



—

The candidate estimated the number of the crowd too high, and was called on it.
The dead were estimated by the minute in real time.
The slippage is dangerous or miraculous, depending on how.
The chorus can slip into only us as the poppies slip in redness.



—

*A crowd today is what can happen in a crowd. A crowd today is what can happen to a crowd.*
She has to begin again by the unaltered slippage of red poppies into _____

13

untroubled by over-determination or fear. We have to believe we are of the thumb
bruising the petal of poppies ourselves and can begin again.

We have to weed ourselves out again of the gallop into form, and then?
She can't quite begin.

—

Stay together, stay together,
says a family in the crowd, they are all flags to each other, their shirts or their hats or
their heights, recognizable internally, like odd sprigs of stray wheat, shooting out
from a field. How many sprigs? *35 clusters of sprigs.*

—

Alertness had grown into fear, already.
It is a depiction of the field.
It is a 19th-century pre-Impressionist depiction of their red blotted proliferation on
the swelling of the field, to which she steps closer for closer resolution.

—

The relation of the abdomen to poppies was a jazz flute riffing.
The breath was made into a step of a crippled man climbing a staircase,
with patience. He climbs both vertically and horizontally like sound.

At the top of the stairs, a single poppy, drooping flat, like a small animal, drowned.

—

How many poppies? *Too many poppies. She can't see herself for the redness of poppies.*

The crowd presses in on itself like the whiteness of
a page and the internal wages against it.
We have to weed ourselves out again of the gallop into form, and then?

—

The woman on the horse is a trajectory through the poppies.
They slipped horizontally, and vertically, more, swaying and shivering, adding tower.
*What do you hope for? What do you hope for?*
The woman has business apart from the flowers.

—

Now we barely see the woman on a horse at the back edge of the poppies,
before the trees begin,
before which the layers of the horizontal rise like swelling seas, or the pushing up
of breath on the chest of a man asleep. He's sleeping fitfully, he's not asleep,

he's less than sleep, or more. He is galloping behind form but toward it.

—

Perhaps the crowd of poppies extends.
Perhaps the crowd of poppies extends from the back of the woman's brain
like the train of a queen's gown.
Perhaps the woman in the black movement on the horse is riding from _____
or riding to _____. Perhaps the woman is the black movement and nothing else.

*10,000 poppies. 10,000,000 poppies. Numerated poppies. She can't quite begin.*

—

The field is a kind of rally for poppies to grow and grow drowsy.
*A crowd today is what can happen to a crowd.*
*A crowd today is what can happen in a crowd.* The poppies were slipping.

We have to begin again with the petal-bruised poppies, their positioning in waves
and lift, the darkness into form and this.

—

*How many poppies?* 10,000 poppies. *How many crowds?* 10,000,000 crowds.
*How many wilting?* Negative 5 wilting.
*How many poppies?* Hope in the shape of poppies. *How many wars?* Estimated hope.
*Were you among the poppies?* She was among imagined poppies.

—

A black movement gallops fitfully, and then…
She was one or 10,000,000 or the incorrect estimation.
She wanted to spread like a thread in a blanket horizontally down over the swells and

sunken dips of the field, trusting poppies as only poppies.

—

The breaths like the hillside rose and fell. The horse continued galloping
behind them.

### *Empty lot*

*—to be read by 2 alternating voices with some pause between*

a.                                                                b.

It was a field
full of weeds
instructing presence.
The presence
of the weeds
signaled absence
of our hands.

*Oblivious seeds,*
*strategic thorn.*

It was a field
full of accidental lace
demanding presence;
The presence
of the war put
more presence on
our hands.

*Oblivious seeds,*
*strategic thorn.*

*Look at your hands,*
*cracked with clearing!*
A bouquet
of leaves
and stems, already limp.

*It's from the field*
*full of weeds*
*instructing presence.*

The hands are tired
from pulling
squid roots,
larger than flowers,
already spent.

*Oblivious seeds,*
*strategic thorn.*

*Torn thistle,*
*news, glove.*
You are too absent
then too present.

*Oblivious seeds,*
*strategic thorn.*

## Slippage and parade

Slippage: the claim
of the Rose Parade Princess unhooked and swaying, partially frozen laugh.
Slippage: in the news, a construction crane that split in half, killing two.
New slippages, appointments of the mind,

pushed off by crisis (the crisis of slippage seldom seen as such).
Instead, a last piece of paper for which we rampage through the papers.
Instead, the rampage of protection against slippage.
For example, a girl must be consoled and fed by a spoon,

or, I fed my eyes the parade.
Other slippages, neither smaller nor larger, loom.
Soon, we will see the mechanical dragon or the dancing horse.
Soon, soon, the mechanical dragon or the dancing horse.

## After *Swan Lake*

I said the bird was not ____(presence splice, desire)
or was and then was not,
that there were multiple birds.
The bird held the dignity of having been turned
and turning:
I said the bird was not ____(love or the cut)
or there were multiple loves.
The legs = the neck. All slope connected tonight
all dignity all threat. The bird was not the neck.
Or there was one love multiplied
cuts. We expected this much:
the neck was not the black swan in gone movements
embedded in us.
We were and then were not
multiple or cut.

We expected this much: the black swan in
gone movements, cut.
Whose love?
Whose and our love?

## Ocean interstice
—for Patrick


to the right of the carriage, the white-capped ocean

to the left of ten years, the ocean starts

to the right, the delphinium stem in the heart

to the left of delphinium blue, a crack in the windshield

to the right of ten years, the historical fact of the sea

in the center of the sea, the counting of years

to the left of the sea, the immaterial carriage

to the left of the carriage, the chorus carrying us

to the left of the chorus, the chorused-to

to the right of ten years, delphinium blue

to the left and the middle, love carrying me over glass

to the right of the glass, did I carry you?

to the left of ten years, did I carry you?

to the right and the middle, the marriage of sands

to the left in the center near the carriage near the stem

in the center of the sea, nine months apart

to the left of nine months, the counting of sands

in the center, the ribs, the carriage of the heat

to the right near the center, the carriage and the heat

to the counting of years, did I carry you?

to the right of the carriage, delphinium blue

to the left of the cracked-glass carriage, the tracks of the chorus

to the right of no sleep, were you carrying me?

to the counting of years, the historical mass of the sea

to the left near the center, the carriage's heat

to the left of the heat, the parting of the carriage

to the right of the counting of carriages, immaterial, centered, askew

to the left in the center near the stem

to the counting of years, love carried through glass

to the right of our arms, the discarded gowns of the chorus

to the left of the sounds of ten years, the chorused-to
to the right of the chorus, ten choruses, two
to the right, through cracked glass, delphinium blue

themes
blue
slippage
chorus

## The tail of a kite

—

The chorus was too general, the chorus was a block
from which we hung, like the tail of a kite.

[*Blue kite. Blue diamond on which a crucifix lay.*]

The chorus advanced generally,
the general stepped down, or the chorus sang of the strategies
for advancement in geometric blocks.

The chorus marched and sang and marched and we were hung from it.

[*I read how much the war, how much a vacation
costs.*] Look at us flutter with our figures.

Look at us dip and hang and be tossed.


—

The chorus and the general force, the chorus and the kite
from which we hung or strung or followed—

A man holds the string
and is assemblage, his sneakers planted in the sand.

The chorus has a life with the wind.
He says, chorus,
you have more life than me. Poor man.
He stepped into the tide by mistake.

The chorus does not just sing, it motions
through its song and must.

[*The tail of the kite was shivering, then straight, then sinuous.*]

—

The day and the days and our lists.
We said goodbye blue kite as if it would vanish.

We wanted a new one.

We wished for the type of advancement that makes possible new choruses.
A dragon kite with teeth of blue,
but who were we humming to, ourselves?

What kind of new distance, distraction, solution
[*a multicolored fish?*]

—

The chorus was too general.
[*Blue diamond, dive, and fray.*]

We called we called a chorus more precise, all of us
singing for precision, in a general din

as of lines in an airport—are you American?
I'm in a line now for numbness or I'm
in a line for better days. There was a sharper song we thought
we remembered but couldn't repeat. How did we hear again?

A Marine's family waits with signs and flags.
*Are you American?*

—

The chorus was a collection of parts like us, poor chorus
hanging.

[*The string fell loose, we pulled it tight. It pulled too tight, we let it loose.*]

Good thing we said goodbye this morning I might
see you later, I might lose someone myself.
The song says move, keep moving or you'll lose
the cliff of air that holds you here.

I repeat the chorus movement up
and forward, somewhat repeated

[condensation on the car window, sometimes slivered frost]

The voice like a toy, tossed and tossed and caught and tossed
again. The white sky sings: *by whom? by whom?*

## Western Crow ballad

The Western Crow I loved the most sent a crow ambassador.
He stood atop a telephone wire and paced until I woke.

Good morning crow ambassador, good morning crow, good morning crow.
What blank sky do you represent, what West too Westward now?

I slammed the window by mistake, the morning crow, the heard crow, cawed:
*your sky's beneath a frozen lake, ideal and yet, unthawed.*

*2.  lily tally*

## Madame Star was tired of noise

*She told the chorus to parcel itself out for the sake of peace.*


We parceled ourselves out to get through the week.
43% would flee to the sea, dive into a conch shell,
and compete with the ocean's memory.
26% would curl like foal fetuses into artillery shells, and sleep.
The percentage of us with small wrists was to hold hands with the percentage of us
with large wrists and float on our backs in the Red Sea.
The percentage of us with salt on our hands would withstand this.
The percentage with birthmarks near their knuckles was to
remain on land. 5% would act as the opera that comes from nowhere
to a mottled stallion, smelling the sand.

## The sun left scripts

The sun left scripts of silver on the reservoir then only water.
The paper offers 101s on war then only paper.
Democracy instructs.
Keep them separate, the silver and the chorus

and ultimately, we'll see and then we'll hear, we said to ourselves.
Silver shiver silver surface, only that.
Silver doesn't ask itself what would it give, give up
or give away; is wouldn't be silver then,

right? It wouldn't be shining
through the center, apparent and profitless and barely white.
The water moving turned to silver for a moment then
to clear again—the sun

on the water turned to silver blinding then to sun.
The sun left scripts of silver on the reservoir then only water.
Pull them apart
without ripping: paper pasted with old glue,

pull the silver from instructions,
take instructions from the permeating silver. We were slivers, then,
of silver, right? Run and run around the reservoir, leaking
profitless, uncaught.

Test silver spoons by tapping the pipes.
Test our days against what they are not.
The silver had white bleeding through the center
like a wound.

The force of sifting out the silver was disaster;
carry the blind spot of faster-into-silver,
as if disaster saves.
The silver had no force of instruction or will, no democracy earned,

no metaphorical derangement.
Around and around the fountain the runners run, the pedals circle.
I am not current anymore beside you silver.
I am not currency, said silver, so leave me here.

## Oregon cherries, and other claims

A new report delineating benefits to the state of things like cherries, rivers:
an economic multiplier effect, a series of expanding orbs around which
dotted stones sunk.

The numbers were in millions like the cherries in the bins.
The numbers were in love with Bing cherries, hearty, thick-skinned,
in love with what they stood for, or withstood, stained pits and all.

We plucked the cherries and ate the numbers and dove in rivers, over and over.
We absorbed the cherries into the river, then, and multiplied
ourselves with them. I doubt the veracity of the report, sang a clerk stacking bins.
We doubt the assumptions in doubt, bled the cherries.
Still, we were absorbed in it, an obsession with reportage or claim
against which the river slipped, over which, or through.

The cherries took the preposition *from* from the river, hung
from gnarled branches, or sequenced from
the weightless blossoms. From everywhere, the river.

Numbers of us hid.
A box rotted in a warehouse, discovered by a clerk batting fruit flies from his face.
The sun laced through the blossoms, where we hid.
We were strangely satisfied at times when something like a raft was pulled out from
under us, to which we had clung,
and we sunk like the stones and swam, in strange gratefulness and fear.

## Flurry series

### 4 choruses

1.

    *[I stood in the chorus accused of lulling—*
    *I stood in the chorus accused of falling—*
    *I stood in the coursing of voices]*


2.

While we have been parented by trees—while we have been a meadow
with a tree line upon it, while we have been a meadow
with a brown doe within it—
while we have been parented by trees, into which we flow and retreat,
the doe turning, while we repeat
blackberry thickets or sleeves of new light—while we have cleared trees
for the theater of meadows—
while we have cleared meadows, cleared cropped limbs from shadows—

    *[while we have been parented by trees,*
    *while we have been lullabied by trees.]*


3.

A chorus sung by Western yards and windows,
a chorus framed by stained camellia blossoms strewn,
a chorus singing less than alleluias,
less than the recycled news in homes—

they didn't sing beheadings, real or comic, no alarms sounding
blossoms against beams, no voices thrown in high notes, pure and manic—
a chorus as a landscaped line, or drone.

4.

The trees transferred choruses
from eaves to branches—from branches to eaves—
in their slippers and gowns, in their suits and linings and cowboy boot
dresses, in prints and in tresses and costumed sounds—


*Let them play without voices a day let them say what they can without voices a day*
said the trees of the forest.

Today was a shift or a transfer of chorus, a voting machine
for illiterate populace—one voice for one marble,
the marbles rolled down.

> *[A voter walks in with his pencil*
> *and leaves with the silence of forests.]*

## Granularity and the chorus

[We are today
some 92%]

Red fire trucks through glass doors—doors the size of fire trucks—
suburban banners for the sake of banners: cartoonish sunrise, frog.
There is not just one there is not just one there are many—

   *What do you like? Who do you like?*

## 1 chorus

At last the chorus laughed at its rows
of oval heads and notes, its ink blots
and wide lips and throats, as if it needed repeatable song to be free—

> *Free as the*
> *free as the*
> *free as we*

The chorus shed its weeping and its pleas.
A black cat sleeping on the upright stack of cardboard boxes
must have been up all night—

> *Quiet, quiet*
says the chorus, quiet says the inhabitable life.

## Chorus repeated too long

With what would you fill it, the valley, the canyon,
with what would you fill it, with black notes, with men?
What would you transfer from valleys to canyons?
What song would you save for the beginning and end?


And what would you sing to the child that you carry?
And what is the chorus repeated too long?

With what would the canyons receive you—what flurry
of snow or of worries would transfer?


What transfer would fill it, the vertical canyon, the cuts and the hollows,
the small rivers down?
What chorus repeated what transferring echo would sound
like the rivers might sound?


With what would you fill it, with what would you fill it,
who cannot yet fill it with sound?

## Chorus's voting guide

Measures of sound
| | |
|---|---|
| 1 | no |
| 1.1 | no |
| 1.11 | no |
| 1.111 | no |
| | tc.    e |

Sound as sand:
"river"
"white"
"olivine"
"sand-colored" –            X

Judge of sound:
| | |
|---|---|
| Water lily – | *corrupt* |
| Water lily – | *corrupt* |
| Reflection of water lily – | *corrupt* |
| Water lily – | X |

## Dreamed Thoreau

I dreamed Thoreau drew frogs all night
on pale paper,
some numbered thousands
of frogs  Think it was a good dream
Say, I had bad or good dreams

Getting at something
what I wanted to say and what it seemed
seeming good.
I dreamed Henry David Thoreau drew
some number
down to the ones
I can't remember   Not the frogs themselves
but the fact of his   attention to them
however          blotched or poison blue
I had no faith

In our yard, an old sink with wet envelopes in it  ·
The sky is a boy in
purplish rags singing

*Thoreau is tied to the frogs, Thoreau is tied to the frogs,*
and the frogs
are singing from the sink:
make it good, try hard

## Swan Island after Swan Lake
—after an announcement of Freightliner layoffs

*—a and b to be read simultaneously*

| a. | b. |
|---|---|
| Count many, or count none, | *1, 2, 3, 4, 5, 6, 7,* |
| count swans, or count knobs. | |
| Count people seeking jobs, | *1, 2, 3, 4,* |
| count reportage, count performances, | |
| repeated, count arched spines or talk. | *1, 2, 3, 4, 5, 6, 7, 8,* |
| Count security cameras | |
| on loading docks: 5, 6, | *1, 2, 3, 4,* |
| property stalking property. | |
| | *1, 2, 1, 2,* |
| | |
| A warehouse mirrors others and collapses, | |
| box after box after box. | *1, 2,* |
| Odelia mirrors sister swans, | |
| or they mirror her, | *1, 2, 3, 4, 5, 6,* |
| the dittoed unmarked necks | |
| sloping out of fog. | *1, 1, 1, 1, 1, 1, 1,* |
| A blue-jeaned figure floats | |
| on the side of the widest road, | *1, 2, 3,* |
| but native to it. | |
| Which the multitude, which the one? | *1, 2, 3, 4, 5, 6,* |
| | |
| A flock of starlings scatter to a gun. | |
| Cough up your food | *11, 12, 13, 14,* |
| to feed your young, or cough up nothing. | |
| I said the swan was not | *1, 2,* |
| the load I carry, | |
| but then she was. | *1, 2* |

## *Devotion and Red Ginger*

The chorus sang
devotion and red ginger
in the stalks
thick as wrists
higher than men

Not a native flower

The chorus sang
devotion as red ginger
blossoms locked
thick as fists
clearer than sense

Devotion knocking
down the stalks
to get to them, too rare
to miss:
arrow cluster, center clutched,
false reds, false flowers

The chorus
crescendoed
terrible beauty like
a machete clearing
all else, all else.

Oh, prehistoric flower,
false interior.

Devotion flattened
down the forest floor:
Red ginger blossoms
then
red ginger blossoms then...

## Chorus inventing lilies

*—italics to be read by a second voice*


1.
The noise reflected a poverty of lilies so we invented lilies.

*Sing the exactitude of lilies*


2.
Devotion and reflection were out of focus, while the lilies were exact.
Devotion and reflection were quiet but lived like always
beside the lilies, the kind
of poverty which does not speak and is not asked.

*We were not just that*


3.
We do not wish to speak of poverty we wish to speak of lilies
which are in poverty, too, as white.

*Tight lilies on the stem*


4.
The chorus directed themselves against noise:
devotion and reflection you are sister lilies floating in the pond.
A salamander's head lifts devotion
only slightly, then dips down.

*Sound out the silt in which we float*


5.
The lily edge a thin film like the last layer of baby diapers.
But in and in the petals
grew dense, and did not bend but broke.

*Take lilies into noise*

6.
The will was a damp blouse wrinkled from being wrung
and hung out of habit.
The word poverty instills a poverty of lilies, sang the chorus,
though its reflections exist, repeated.

*I am not reflected in that*


7.
Reflection, say: sounds
are making circles around and beneath us.
Devotion: you are the softest kick, the movement of a fetus.

*Less than us the lilies*


8.
The chorus was dressed in white robes to revert to the flowers, with
hooded heads and open mouths.

*Might be from poverty*


9.
We sang to poverty, you are not louder than the lilies, but as a taunt.
You are the blue curve of the lip.
I can sing of the tip of you, but barely.

*Fill the cracked glass with lilies*


10.
You are no soldier of poverty you are no soldier of devotion sang the lilies.
There were children among the lilies wrapped in devotion.

*One of them a lily*

11.
They were not just white pale blue pale pink bled from their centers.

*We were not just poor*


12.
The cobra lilies reflected wealth while Peruvian lilies reflected lukewarm
waters… we reflected our own impatience, then,
and were ashamed.

*name the Peruvian name for lily*


13.
Reflection and devotion were cobra lilies hissing against each other
until the footsteps tamed them.

*Devotion rose as noise*


14.
Plastic lilies in the middle of a mall beside which a girl and mother argue.
Lilies flung from brides' wrists flying
Someone dying in the way that joy is said to die, unwritten.

_____*die unwritten*


15.
Footsteps of a woman carrying a child on her hip
through bruised petals, the child swaddled in white.

*Might be from lilies*


16.
Voices sword-fought lilies cupping air, someone leapt and leapt and wept
to get at lilies.

*We were not just fight*

17.
Poverty did not mean noise nor did a sword mean silence.
Those who did not want to hear the noise tried to move away
but broke branches as they went.

*So they are not just lilies*


18.
The chorus repeated
*lily lily lily* until the noise of it was harmless, and the reflection of the chorus
shivered in us.

*A stem too long*


20.
Light blue light pink bled from their centers.

*Repeating was psychosis and a song*

## Pine

[Caught, centuries,
identifying

pine needles]

[rinds dropped
among pine needles]

[blood drying
in pine needles]


[buck, bird, or man]

[branches misaligned
in their curvatures
cupping and
cracking, amongst or

between needles]

[among or between us,
needles rusting]

[Whitebark, Winter,
Western White]

[point upon point upon
point]
[line up, line up!]

*3. Lola, backstage*

## The chorus backstage

cries:
the performers are not there, just a stage for their mistakes, an estival lilac air

that curves around the thigh, around the back, around
the thigh. [Enter, actors undressing, folded hands familiar hands, turning

globe, quiet tantrum.]
Here, our whitish gowns to shape disaster; gowns scorched for sake of color.

The actors disembody their own voices. Why would we crave it, then,
the body's dissolution, having come from there?

[Enter: turning globe, lobed shadow, knowledge of love in darkness. Enter:
having come from there.] I came from dissolution, sang.

We came from dissolution, sang. [Enter, familiar hands in darkness,
tickets for nonmembers, plastic cup of fizz-water, desolation dissolution touching.]

[Enter, but I came from there.] Dissolution costs, we said, we fell from that,
a test. [Enter, performance, burn-pink sky, a looking sideways now for love,

form, cormorant.] Now keep looking at the stage,
turning, green globes and darkness.

## The chorus backstage, 2

Have you dressed yet, Miss Horizon, on what stage will you be traced?
How much skin and how much costume in your gown, burn-pink and laced?

Where's your dress now, Miss Horizon, in what revolving case?
Where's your skin and where's your costume, what direction should we face?

Where's your entrance, Miss Horizon, what direction does it face?
Where's your skin, where's your costume, what your skin, what your costume?

Have you guessed yet, Miss Horizon, in what turns are you effaced?
How much burn becomes your costume, how much pink in which you're lost?

## The sunset is a catastrophe to yellow

The sunset is a catastrophe to yellow, but yellow is the base of it.
I am a catastrophe to myself, or I am myself.

The slippage that we must avoid is a certain blanketing in which
the delicacy of perception is lost.
A small degree of slippage and yellow is the cost of oblivion, the eyes delving in.


Excessive slippage and the "homeless man" living in
a tent on the street is an example of
"homeless man" and the street is an emblem of the street.

A small amount of slippage and the wrens surmised by catch of movement
in the camellia bush appear, the yellow above them unimaginably near.

Excessive slippage and the camellias are men shaking
in piles of petal blankets, absorbed in rage and fear.

Excessive slippage and I am the yellow egg dye, taking over, unnaturally so.
Excessive, and the words have spines and nerves that overtake what's here.
Excessive slippage and the man who becomes president
in a black suit is an example of
"president" and the suit is an emblem of a suit.


Catastrophic orange blots the land.
Myself is fantastic to the spirit, but spirit is the face of it.
America is fantastic to myself, but is not the base.

The election is an embellishment of yellow, though pillows itself in hope.
The sunset is a catastrophe to yellow, but yellow is the base of it.
I am a catastrophe to myself, or I am myself.

Night we fight our own catastrophes or our tendency to dive there.

I took off the layer of yellow.
I took off a layer of silt.

A just enough slippage, and a child slips onto a lap or a knee.
A just enough slippage, and the words and the men do not flee
from one another. A freezing man rejects a gift of wool socks, rejecting
the "give to the homeless" box.
America is a fantasy or America is a catastrophe of given talk.

A small amount of slippage and I heard the sound of the child's patting footsteps
on the stairs, coming down.
The slippage we must avoid is a blanketing of yellow interference, crowning all.

Who are you, camellias?
You fall to the base of yourself.

The slippage we must avoid is the blotched and blotching bush,
the blanketing in which the two wrens are swallowed in cry, or
swaddled men are swallowed and blanketed in hunger and cuss.

Oblivion is a violence done to perception, and perception is a violence
done to sunsets and men and camellias, falling brown and apart.

Say, sunset must rhyme misfit
or yellow is not a base at all of the sunset, but a symptom.

The sunset is a factory of misfit shades, curling and re-curling.

## Abandon reflection

—after differing translations of Federico García Lorca's *Balcón*, by
Carlos Bauer and W.S. Merwin


Lola who is formed of light:
*"Lola who would look at herself so much in the pool"*—or
*"Lola who looked so long at herself in the pool"*—which is she?
Frequency or length? Vanity or night?
A stream of light came down on Lola or her reflection there,
where she was pooled
Say: abandon reflection in place of something unhinged
from the pool, "so much" or "so long"
Lola who is formed of light: her white fingers in the water breaking water
Lola's blank light streaming
I stand in a corner store in which
faces glisten in magazine light
The city is pooled in mirrors and young girls glance
at themselves in pieces here

## The chorus as template

[*Begin.*] There was a soldier template in the grass, he
bent and lifted it, being not a soldier.

[*Begin.*] There was a man behind the template
in salute, there was a template of impersonation,
mask and all, there was a 9/11 firefighter mask,
there was an Iraq veteran mask, there was the lifting
of a clover by which a man is cast as clover.

[*Begin.*] There was a soldier template in the grass, beside
the clover, overgrowing, fast-entangled.

[*Begin.*] The hands over the ventricles of the heart
and the anthem and the podium, there was
the straight from zero to soldier-dome despite
the charge and lie, there was the typifying
jaw, the dewy distant eyes, there was objection
casting clover in overcast and cries.

[*Begin.*] Beneath cumulonimbus, beneath combat, beneath
new growth and clover, beneath the last helicopter lost
and the casting votes and crowd, the noise
of the audience was roaring, roaring, loud.

[*Begin.*] When the actual theater itself came loose,
inflaming actual soldiers, with eyes, their own eyes,
un-templated and fast, inflaming charges for the man
who stole ____ and ____ and ____ .

[*Begin.*] There were soldiers, actual soldiers, not actors, in the grass,
there were bees becoming soldiers,
there was grass and grass and more grass.

## Lola, America
—after Woody Guthrie lyrics and *Balcón*, Lorca


1.
Lola imagines non-Lola by the lake
over herself, over herself
skipping off reflection or
some kind of ant that doesn't care
other ants or soil.
Lola looking tilted in the water
protect and what she needs to protect
or not, to count.
*Hey Lolly Lolly Lo;*
*la la* generic song
by *l-l-l-*
the water hears her.

lily-walking on the water
like some kind of water skipper

what it stands on,

wonders what counts enough to

Close the eyes, cry the lilies.
Lola a name and a sound like *la la*
fixed
of water as if

### Discontinued chorus

Do you remember Gumby?
Where did it come from?
Do you remember yourself?
Do you remember the chorus?

Say it is faceless
and blue like the rubber Gumby doll held by the feet & flung,
its wrist-like waist bending too far
its blank spoon-handle neck, swinging back, remembering
atrocity is like that:


[not Gumby, not eraser]—who is erased?


a chorus faceless but with planted feet,
a discontinued, yet existent chorus, squealing chants
with conscience, rights with tonsils, till        .

their gleam-blue, price-tagged foreheads lean without you, toward you, almost
touching clay or spade
or concrete—

## Experiment with seven hearts

Try your heaven in the attic
your taxidermic static
cloud
Let in starlings, let in publics,
see what they do

The presences impart
heavens anew

Try your heaven automatic
Try your condemned lace-work
heaps of heaven
your emphatic
trying
presence in my seven hearts

Try now seven seasons static
in the streets
Let eleven teenage, walking, wearing headphones
Let in deafen,
amp and prison, see what they do

Take your heaven from the attic
Let in missiles and fanatics
Let in starlings pecking sunflower hearts
Let in failure, pushing
carts
The presences impart
presences anew

Try seven routes up and up past ancient attic
heavens, past removal and transaction,
past the papers
creased
with fold, protecting
news: beheadings, keeping it news

Try your starlings flying, erratic
Let infusing voices climb the
ladder
to a barely-light,
seven-heart
quiet, see what they do

# anniversaries walking
—*to be read by 27 voices* —→ intention?

a

Singing "I'm not being a monkey" makes the child seem monkeyish. Saying I can't think of it, what do you think of? The anniversary of being being the anniversary of not being that, a negative space caught.

b.

The anniversary of seeing children swinging from trees remembering swinging from trees is at heart a bleed of anniversaries. If you were born Christmas Day you share a birthday with Isaac Newton and Sissy Spacek simultaneously. Inlets bleed.

c.

The anniversary of being drawn simultaneously with a leaf in the sun, where the leaf is contained in you, the anniversary of being born by loving leaves, where you are leaving yourself constantly.

d.

Yesterday not simultaneous to today, though a loved love is all ages of himself simultaneously. A monkey's eyes meet a child's eyes at a zoo, simultaneous to time nodes breaking apart in you.

e.

Liquidity wherein you speak yourself as 2-somes or as 3-somes or as 1-tone simultaneously sung, strung from millions or from chromosomes or seeds.

f.

The 10-year anniversary of 9/11 broadcast and rebroadcast, naming numbers of the dead together, what's able to be integrated, what was never, simultaneously severed and compressed and renewed—

g.
People opening and parting inside people, people needing what they're not, or people dreaming what a flock is not imagining.


h.
Undrawn things. Soldiers losing tongues for example, tragedy, simultaneous to memories of children laughing reckless with some firecracker strings.


i.
Babies being born simultaneously close to New Years, one of them the New Year's Baby.


j.
Yesterday the harbor exploded for example yesterday the reef was finger-colored and green. She flitted through, not fitting in herself exactly.


k.
A monkey is a funny thing with eyes. Cries are funny things to monkey with. Simultaneous to newborn children crying, other children, beating piñatas open, blindfolded.


l.
People numbering lost people, convoluted, effecting node integration, simulation of the claw in left-brained sense flaws—scratched and fluted.


m.
Someone asked us to give someone a lucky number, like giving a goose its own tail feather, then luck and bad luck switched hands and walked, which was something you didn't talk about.


n.
She spoke simultaneously with someone being stuck in a hole and someone's birth and someone shouting at a screen.

o.

To be depleted by what you are or what you are not, caught mid-harbor,
distractedly or partially, to eat is to smell is to think, for example, to feel is to
broadcast, to drink—


p.

Who wants to swing from a tree as herself anymore? Who wants to sleep as
numbers funneling into sea? Who wants to sleep as Angelina Jolie? Who wants to
be walking through leaves, anymore? You'd have to be an anniversary walking.


q.

She wants to purchase order by purchasing simultaneously selfhood and bleed, she
wants to order 10 sheet-sets and 30 pillows, and fill the beds with glistening seeds.


r.

Someone at the memorial speaks the names of the dead simultaneously, voices
touching voices effecting nodes, from which water flows forward, from which
lives flow backward—glistening.


s.

Fingers glisten when you lick them, lick off sugar lick off salt—


t.

A firefighter in the North Tower thought the voices he heard were voices of the
dead having died together being on the other side, before he realized he was alive.


u.

Imagine it's the undrawn night. The anniversary of no seizure was a light.


v.

Imagine spider monkeys crying, their eyes more wet than people's eyes. Imagine
people pantomiming death, then imagine people dying.

w.

The news is on, the news is on at the same time as the game, sorry, it's on at the same time, I'm sorry.


x.

If you were born today, you share a birthday with neural candles lit, you share speaking with a cast, you share a birthday with Loretta Swit who was Hot Lips on *M\*A\*S\*H*.


y.

Families speaking loudly simultaneously so hearing nothing. A seizure unrepeated, but re-broadcast, unreduced.


z.

Being repeated chime and crime and love and people touching other peoples' suits. Each day drawn in nodes untouched, climbing God's trees, loose.


a.

Simultaneous to her, the thought of her in real time—which even she can think about—sideways, through a flute.

## Island remnant

I carved a miniature horse out of wax. The wax was meant to coat a surfboard
cracked where the chest would lay, a misshapen cube left on stacks of towels.
I carved a miniature horse from it. I couldn't carve exact
but made the nostrils and the eyes and the flat of the nose the hands might pet,
but tiny hands. The horse was small and smelled of coconut oil.

I carved him with a paperclip and spoon.
My opulent tiny moon horse, his nostrils too big, mane too coarse,
but it could have been worse.
*Of course the ocean took the fields. It took the childhoods and the fields.*

## Lola's pools

So listen the lions, they were not just lions.
They were not just lions, they were not just fed.
So listen, the sounds, they were not just round.
*They were not just poor. She was not just beautiful. They were not just beheaded.*

\*

So listen, the chorus. They were not just florid,
they were not just crescendo, they were not just alliance or silken or vetted.
So listen, the lions they were not just defiance they were not just
lying in heaps like everything said.

So listen the votes, her votes, they were not just fleeing her water-head,
floating, they were not just flatter, dark-matter, or scratches of lead.

\*

*I dreamed of the weight of the paws of the lions, forgotten in sleep like a boy, getting older.*
So listen, the soldiers, they were not just molded from beauty or
stutter, they were not just unhinged and fetal and folded, she had not
just told her own head that it's lying about them, knows nothing, is cruel.

\*

So listen the lions, their heads were cut off
to attest to *they're lions.*

\*

*All murderers, all lies, and all fools appeared likewise in liquid, oblong sections.*
*Everyone speaking spoke in dissections.*
So listen, the pools, they were not just pools.

**4.** *yellow, yellow, yellow*

# [untitled]

The moon saw the cavities of Rome
I skirt from thing to thing
*Good morning young prince*
A loon or a moon in a goodnight song
I dreamed the inherited West
Good morning young prince
Too soon
too soon
Who are your inheritors?
Cavities in the ruins
sparrows in the cavities
ashes in the sparrows

*same line, different presentation*

## The 4th

*Who inherited fire displays? Or inherited first?* The dream drops explode and
we like the others receive them toward us.

The neighbor children stand in line and shoot Roman Candles counting backward
before they start then forward once they shoot,
to 5.

One girl is all skirt against the darkness and twirls around unhurt in it.

We sing of inherited freedom who inherited night as we inherited purple strings
vanishing from past wars.

Or, the neighbor children stand in line and shoot Roman Candles counting
5-4-3-2-1 before
they start, then 1-2... with each flare, to 5. We sing of the pale of the skirt.
*Who inherited backward?*

themes
inherit
cavity

## Sponsored roses

The roses were free because they were sponsored.
The sponsors' roses were gold-leafed, dipped and stained by the sponsors.

Some actual machine or, maybe, hand, dipped them, cool-dried, into it.

The gold was a color meaning gold.


The rodeo court wore gold-sequined hats and flashed by, meaning only that.

The sponsors' advertisements waved in the wind and then, "inalienable gold,"
the literal rose, a given trademark unfolding.

We rose to clap at real but sponsored roses unveiled to the anthem singer,
or most, I think all of us, rose.


The recipient of sponsored roses dedicated them to good morning soldiers.
They were actual roses for actual soldiers then, or they were causes to
proliferate roses. Or they were still roses, on the interior

verdant, gold-leafed and dipped. A man was kicked in the head.


A person can be sponsored too. A mother pointed out to a boy the flags
in the wind. *Good morning, good morning, good morning,* I said.

The sponsors were endorsed by the partners of the roses
and the endorsements of injuries waved.
The roses were dried red, but also gold.

Take what you want. They were free, except for the goldness.

## Inherited travel

*"Traveling is sentimental"* —Lyn Hejinian


—You've inherited movement today, good morning young prince:
    still joy in the eye.
—You've gotta see the Gorge while you're here.
—You've gotta eat a ____ while you're here.
—Ends up the world of the stomach contains "gotta" and "you got to"
    and Coliseum tours, the sewers an inheritance as much as the crows.
—Pick it up here and lift, and lift, and lift, sick with the scent of ourselves,
    driving away.
—An American family talks of the Borghese:
    "The family was pretty well-to-do, I guess."
—See, we might in sickness, sick with the scent of the war, driving away.
—See, we might through Oregon, driving through Columbia River Gorge
    see: The Dalles, the melting of the two lls at night.
—Rome still here, syntax-less, crawling forward like a beetle, misshapen,
    flat-headed, leaving the mind, and the mind the pale sugar
    slightly specked with bits of the beetle's antennae.
—You've inherited movement today,
    small movements of the string legs of insects.

## Roman Oaks

The oaks sprout up, sprout up and up.
The immediacy of breath will test us, then, what's left?

The immediacy of oaks tower over breath.

## Roman Forum lemons

The observance of the crime became a crime: top-down, or stemming up,
like a tree, in which the tourists are the frays of leaves, rustling.
The crime continued in continuance.
We tour the stones where Christians were tortured and
continue past, casually aghast.

The argument continues over waterboarding, where did it stem from,
and continue? Here is the top-down hanging fruit. Here are the lemon trees
with lemons hanging over. We would like to not continue here.
We are tortured by the perfection of the lemons.

## The earphones and *La Verità*
—after the unfinished sculpture, Gian Bernini, Museo Borghese, Rome


—Something in truth left grotesque and we're best so


—Before she turned from marble to truth,
   the nipple was connected to the thumb with a glue or a gum, a stretched
   string, but of marble...


—Something slipped off the breast of *La Verità*, the nipple connected to the thumb
   with a glue or a gum but of marble, and

   the rock from which the marble chunk had come, gutted with blank space
   (the slippage begins us then)—but we're best so


—*I'm hot* or *I'm cold. Buy some earphones, buy some gum* (apricot light, morning come)
   *I'm someone* or *I'm stone* or *I'm one* or *I'm none...*


—Strength the length of unfinishing, strength the length of the words uttered in
   streams of sun.


—Before we turned into people turning, something in truth barely true.
   Someone coughs conspicuously. Someone's born within a glance and, still, her
   breast and her thumb, connected,

stretched fat, undone.
*Am glue or am gum  Am hot or am cold*, says she, holding a shell or a sun


—Strength the length we can hold her in thought before the mind's turning again
and gone (the slippage begins us again, morning come)


— "the key is that she is seated"
or "she is the sex of the marble" the slick cavity unfinished tending toward
sex or toward stone.


—The people are barely here.
Words and marble barely reference a shade of stained molars or bone
(we have to begin again, morning come)
(the margin begins us again, morning light)


(apricot on marble)


—Note:
Both the places for slippage and rampage hold and yet the nipple still connects to
the thumb, the error undone

## The raindrop story

We make a story of alligator/gladiators:

*from where the raindrops? I ran then—*

You and the non sequitur—why?
Do we so distrust what is given that—healthy wariness so that—
the delicacy remains—but not distrust, or yes—distrust.
*What does the raindrop want of us?*

Say: the alligator gladiator crawled into the sky.
Say: abandonment, war, error, you and the terror of positioning or lie.

Consider the need to trust then too.

### *The abdomen was the mountain...*

The tourists were their abdomens continuing.
The tourists continued despite the positions from which they continued.
The language continued despite the positioning from which it cavitied.
The abdomen the cavity of the trunk below the diaphragm usually including the
pelvic cavity, the abdomen the cavity out of which... what are you?
Continue over the forum peeling an orange.
Continue tour-guide, continue tone.

The abdomen was the mountain, over which the people continued
walking, with breath alone. The abdomen as continuance, the liquid fruit,
the funeral dirge, pan-handler fountain. The abdomen the mountain on which
the tourists breathe in shallow threes and twos.
Blue of rotten fig and breath, with death in the air again: reported death.
Breath that doesn't choose what to breathe, breathing bus perfumes and
something left in words and glue. What are you? A campaign?
What's a flower? Another tourist?
There are cavities of air inside an orange.
There are cavities of people inside people.

# Regions

Regions of mountains then regions of less,
regions of distrust then regions of softness
Goof morning young leaf
Good morning young thief
Good morning young hollow in the torn yellow fruit

America, a soft-skinned prince inheriting

itself, regions of intent
then regions of reach, overreach,
then regions of quench
Good morning good morning good morning young speech
Regions of trust then region of disgust with our trust   softness, softness

Regions of the abdomen rising and falling in speech.

## The tour of the abdomen of *La Verità*

I called the abdomen the abdomen. I called myself a tourist. I called myself myself.
The nipple still connected to the thumb, unfinished still, unchipped, undone,
and if we tour her then unfinished sum.


If we tour ourselves each day, a foreign form, the way we tourists tour
in headphones, stopping here, on cue, and moving, cued, along—

If we stay a little longer than we should, and fall behind
to something, here, a guilt or snag, or something far, the plastic of a scar.


If I tour the day I die, unfinished still,
there is no atrocity of breath, at last and less.

body as scape

## Yellow Lake

—Yellow Lake, a paint pigment made at times from crushed buckthorn berries

I've inherited state highway signs for Blue Lake, overlaid by the abstract
Yellow Lake, swapped or replaced.
I've inherited Blue Lake, I thought, caught in traffic, too late.
What are you waiting for?

Yellow Lake an unused paint, painting nations, a station obliterating destination.
There were women waiting like me—the women were in response
to their waiting, existing as a function of their own waiting, and they
rebelled from that.

I inherited Yellow Lake today, a blind spot in the mirror in which
the worlds approach simultaneously,
without function, in one shade. Who inherited you, water?

Yellow Lake spoke like a teenager speaks in absolutes held up in relation.
Yellow Lake was a station of heaven.

Meanwhile, the drivers in response to their waiting, existing as a function
of their own waiting, rebelled from that.

They inherited Yellow Lake, crushed buckthorn berry, becoming or obliterating
anything, what were they waiting for? The shape of their rebellion took
a color not a lake, it was a shade used
to display sun shake on water dripping from that fire.

The children too, those existing as a function of time, layering forks and spoons,
rebelled from that and threw some unburned birthday candles in to be swallowed
*yellow, yellow, yellow* and were akin to it, giggling.

Once upon a time today we lace our speech with Yellow Lake.

There was a freedom without atrocity or reduction, we said anything we wanted
to say forever. Oh summer, un-blue, uncalled for, come—
simultaneous sap, freeway numbness, buckberry, bee pollen fire.

The people existing as a function of reducing, and the people existing as a function
of reduction rebelled too and collapsed and grew
thick, immediate and new in Yellow Lake.

## *Arbitrarily*

—I called myself myself though stemless. The river continued as a river,
arbitrarily named Quench Root or Quartz Fork, an American name or claim,
part personal, part vanished.

—I called the river something though. It was like taming a starling.

—Starling, starling, speckled night, yellow pecking mouth and knife, the name
slipped into, over other names and we became, on the continent, continued.

—I called myself effaced, I called myself displacement then. I called myself
a leaf or fin.

—No name so call it Quench Root, stained as if with chimney soot,
swollen, swollen stem.

*5. office of water*

## Oregon interstice

1.
Between the dash and
the glass, a screwdriver
(its yellow-, black-
and red-striped handle).

2.
Between the original
speech and the turn
of speech,
the front page.

3.
Between this orchard and
the next
orchard,
a tumbled peach.

4.
Between the handling
of questions and the turning neck
of the driver,
the picked-clean orchard.

5.
Between the turning
into peaches and
the red truck,
the original flower.

## Two tigers walking different directions through bamboo

I loved the chorus best when it was two
tigers walking different directions through bamboo,
when one paused,
and the other heard the first, and knew.

No, I loved the chorus best when
there were two, or it was two, one or the other, two or less.
I loved the chorus best when it like
festivities ended, and we were left this morning,
and not a chorus.

Last night at the bar: two fighting, two watching the same screen,
two shooting darts, two claiming chairs, murmuring
of what choruses murmur in the dark smoke, what do you know
that you could tell me?

The chorus was at its best when heaven was a vest
with two sides to button and fall into, held tighter in the chest,
and only slightly warmer...*no.*

The tigers were the quiet of the two
in proximity, sensing each other's movement
and presence, walking forward or back,
to the river water, restless.

The chorus was at its best when one undressed
for the other in the dark,
which was a window
where starlings and sirens grew.

We talked and talked
and stairways fell away, and dart boards fell away,
and starlings fell away,
and all the subjects of the song.
If the tigers came in twos, we walked

between and within each other's sounds,
until we drowned difference out
and the bamboo and the town.

## water at night

What is your office?
Office of water

Water at night
night of black oxen

Dewdrops in eyes
eyes of black oxen

Water is different
different at night

Crickets in office
office of heaven

Heaven iced over
over the water

Water is different
different at night

Different from what?
What is not water?

Heaven from what?
Eyelid from matter

Office of eyelids
eyelids of oxen

Grass beneath oxen
oxen of water

Water is indifferent
Difference becomes it

What is your office?
Oxen and crickets

## Kelp chorus

They are all throat in the night—they say the word *spirit* with ease
They are the drifting, violet gowns of the throat
They are all night in the throat—they are all ease in the all
They say the words *blue* and *baleen* and *sailing* and *seas*
Perhaps they have the relationship of the throat determined and so are all it
Or, they have the slick violet gown of the throat and they are the luster of the gown
slipping over the fragile, wet word of the spirit
Or, perhaps the word *spirit* with ease is the same as the throat
Or, the naked "they" is the same as "they say"

Then we want it divulged, what they have, or had, or seem to have in ease,
a sea of violet gowns washed up in small pathetic heaps,
they are all heaped in the white, coughed up on salt-encrusted sand,
iridescent froth sticking or popping against them
At the touch of the bubble, an acid hurt
Then we are all them, and not without ease

### they say the word *porous*

they say the words *deploy*
and *coding* and *spirit* and *cease*
they say the words *forests*
and *porous* and *humvee* and *cede*

as if all the same
all the same light
as if all the same
*fighting* through *leaf*

*morse code* and *night*
light at the center
*missions* and *moats*
*courses* of battles courses of *choruses*

*notorious light*
tight in the throat
as if all the same as if all the same
[might be the throat

coding the night
might be the forest
porous the voice
coursing the quiet

light pulping through]
they say the words *mulching*
and *marching* and *missile* and *through*
[who were you then?

coughing off light
might be the forest
might be the chorus]
you were *of course I am*

stemming from this
might be the missile
missing the night
you were *of course I'm not*

stemming from this
[forcing light quiet
might be the forest
rescuing leaf]

## Starlings for the election season

*—to be read by 2 voices*


A ragged noise: un-theatric, interspersed,

a forceful wind first through a starling's feathers then the ears.
The noise was not comprised of starlings or the chorus.
We held our feet to this: a plywood platform carrying childhood scents.
The ropes swayed, the sounds muddied and the noise below the chorus grew.


*Look up Dissolution, Bloodied Feet, Frayed Rope, look up Noise from which a Starling Flew.*


There were ropes connected to our throats
and our throats held notes out, so we held by each other's throats; how else
could we have held?


*Look up Nests of Hair for Starlings, throats constricted.*

The candidates chanted at and from us in ill chorus, tossing yellow fibrous ropes.

people n people


*There were People Scratching Votes around the platform… look up People… look up
White Rag Silhouettes on Platforms leaning inward… look up Songs Shaped like Rags
leaning inward… look up Tags Pasted on the Platform… look up Form of Looking Up…
look up Looking; look up Platform-Dusting Rags or Action look up Ragged Stage-lit People*


The starling sang: separate out the platform from the chorus.
*Separate out the chorus from the noise… separate us.*
Not quite impervious but existent and in that, the white gowns upright,
the nests of hair, contest the dissolution into noise.

93

Not quite impervious but existent
and in that, the platform hung suspended, unquiet within us.


*Separate form of looking up. Separate acting without looking.*

They pressed their fingers to their ears like us;
they were acting just like people, but their silk gowns shone sun-radiant in
the stage light unlike staged gowns.



It was Spring; there were Starlings in the Branches,
the young with black-speckled breasts.


*Look up Childhood's Candidate, Nesting Schedule, look up Usurped Silken Sound.*


The platform crashed to the ground, the plywood splitting, a crack, then
done, gone. *Separate accident from will.*
The gowns became rags then.

## 4 rains

*"All human desire is poised on an axis of paradox, absence and presence its poles..."*
—Anne Carson

1.

You were the presence of the rain in proportion.
You were the presence of the rain in proportion to our blood.
What proportion of the rain is needleless, unheard? I can't walk without

your spine slipped into my shirt, sang the chorus.
What proportion of the chorus is the rain?

2.

You were the presence of the rain in proportion.
You were the presence of the rain in proportion to our blood.
And if happiness bit, like a scorpion bites the foot, is the venom a
proportion of the rain? You were the presence of the scorpion in the sun.

3.

You were the presence of the rain in proportion.
You were the presence of the rain in proportion to our blood.

Presence and proportion, reflection and distortion—more—the pheasant
and the scorpion, torque and war and emotion—more—sensation and
devotion, it should all be there.

4.

You were the presence of the rain in proportion.
You were the presence of the rain in proportion to our blood.
If we could only remember the good. Overpresence took the rivers, took
the groundwater up and up—overpresence resulted in forgetting.

# A series of snapping points or rips
—Crater Lake, Oregon

The question of change
is a question of what we can afford to continue.
A series of snapping points or rips.
The lake is a question
of what the mountain can take or not.
The chorus afforded blue, but barely.
The chorus of blue sang out of thin voices
in oxygen-thin air.
The blue vibrated electrons in water and absorbed
what was not turned back.
We turned our backs on the war.
The chorus of blue tilted into our eyes,
and filtering, taught us to filter, but out what?
The chorus of blue held itself up,
a mirror of itself, fanatic and fantastic.
Abstract blue—a new coin—took the center
through, through.
We turned our backs on the lake.
A series of snapping points or rips.
The chorus filtered out disturbance,
filtered out detail and violence
and observance.
*Tilt, shine, tilt…*

What did we shed again, and why?
A little girl wouldn't stop
sobbing, who had to leave
the clearest sky.

## Lola and canoe

The day she is not there, there is a canoe, there was a canoe.

The lines of the canoe, like the dip then lateral stroke of the oars that move it, forward through are the same. The canoe says: the infant splash of the oars entering the water was yours, your love was yours, *remember*.

## *Running sentences*

*—to be read by 3 voices with little silence in between*

a    The chorus is making sentences now: look.

b    A cloud of gnats through which the body like a hailstorm blew.

c    Here in the pockets of the path, there a heaven I avoid.

b    Runners move through gnats, whole bodies move, disrupting.

a    The challenge now is how God moves among appropriating voices.

c    The chorus is making sentences now: look.

b    The trees hold silver plaques naming trees.

a    Every word to screen or paper every binding plaque or structure concerns movement.

b    Little plaques, little sacks of bones coughed up by owls.

c    The challenge now is how the body like a label moves.

b    An oak tree was dismembered and in its place a temple built.

c    A temple was disfigured and in its place a chorus filled.

a    The chorus is making sentences now: look.

b    Here our movement, here the grass.

a    Here in pockets of the path, there a heaven I avoid.

b    The body like a hailstorm blew.

c    Runners move through gnats, whole cities move, disrupted.

a    I was paid to make a sentence today: look.

b    I'm ok in oak or A-OK the little acorns, helmets off and fallen.

c    We play oak men, lost in twigs.

b    Lost or less, appropriation plays approximation plays with centers, ovens, fields.

a    We can make a sentence about oaks, or look at all the sentences on God.

b    Approximated oak trees, fig trees, blank trees stood with plaques.

a    I was paid to make a sentence today: look.

c    A chorus sings in swarms of gnats.

b    First the body on the path, but first the body as circumference.

a    First the cloud of gnats first the movement through the cloud and then the body, not a cloud.

| | |
|---|---|
| c | Look: I'll cook a dinner wrapped in fig leaves. |
| a | Look: I'll make a hillside wrapped in sod. |
| b | Appropriating voices love their figs. |
| c | Here in pockets of the path, there a heaven I avoid. |
| b | The chorus itself mistook us, in our place an oak tree grew. |
| c | The chorus like a hailstorm blurred. |
| a | Every word to screen or paper every binding plaque or structure concerns movement. |
| b | Every mark of wood or labor every sentence, fact, or structure concerns clouds. |
| a | The chorus is making sentences, now: look. |
| c | A city's sentenced to its choruses now: look. |
| b | Here our movement, here the grass. |
| c | Little facts in the chorus, sacks of voice dug up from files. |
| a | The challenge now is how the body as circumference moves. |
| b | The challenge now is how God moves where bodies move, disrupting. |

## The chorus late

The property of the spirit is expanse.
The property of the chorus is a dot.
Or vice versa.
The property of the voice is ownership.
The property of ownership is overwrought.
Or vice versa.

The chorus forgot the lyrics so they made up something on the spot.
*Yellow yellow, hollow hollow.*

A yellow bird, flashing forth, a flower's fur, the sounds came out like
dandelion seeds in wads incanted or dispersed.

*What course occurred outside of voice? Who fought?*
The lyrics backed away from the chorus, backed off to a forest like living things do.

## Acknowledgments

Many thanks to the editors of the following journals and publications in which versions of poems from this book first appeared:

*Burnside Review; Chicago Review; c_L newsletter; Free Verse; Jack London is Dead: Contemporary Euro-American poetry of Hawai'i* (Tinfish Press); *Peep/Show: a Taxonomic Exercise in Textual and Visual Seriality; Pleiades; Quarterly West; The Oregonian; Verse; VOLT; Yew Journal*

Gratitude to Cole Swensen for selecting this collection for the Omnidawn Open Poetry Book Prize. Thank you to Omnidawn editors Rusty Morrison and Ken Keegan for their profound commitment to Omnidawn authors, to Peter Burghardt for his very attuned design of this book, and to all of the Omnidawn team for their wonderful work. Thank you to artist Betty Merken for her generous permission to use the image of her painting *Ascent* for the cover of this book. Many thanks to all friends and colleagues who read and responded to this collection in progress. Gratitude in particular to Mary Szybist for her friendship and insightful, careful reading of these poems at every stage, and to my husband Patrick Playter Hartigan for his clear eye and anchoring support through many revisions. Thanks to friends who read drafts with me at various readings including the Portland Polyvocal Poetry Festival which helped me to hear them and continue. Thanks to the poets in the Spare Room collective for their friendship and making my ears rich with readings, and also to the writers and artists of 13 Hats, and artist Linda Hutchins for generative conversation and collaboration. Thanks to Stephanie G'Schwind and all at Colorado State, Center for Literary Publishing for publishing my first book and the conversations fostered. Thank you to Patrick for his love and belief, for making possible a trip to Rome which prompted some of these poems, and for helping me orient the compass to the next poem, always. Thank you to our son Jackson Thoreau Hartigan for all that he teaches me, and for his kindness, including his gift of a certain Thomas Edison poster just at the right time. Thanks to my parents and four sisters, for their supportive presence. And thank you to all who have been near to me or whose work has been near to me over the course of writing this book, for worlds.

# Notes

Cover
The image on the book cover is from the painting *Ascent* by artist Betty Merken. Please see copyright page for more information.

Epigraph and "Abandon reflection"
The book epigraph by Federico García Lorca is an excerpt quoted from *Balcón* (Balcony). The poem "Abandon reflection" includes excerpts from this poem in two different English translations by W.S. Merwin and Carlos Bauer. *Balcón* is from *Poema del cante Jondo*, copyright Herederos de Federico García Lorca, *Obras Completas* (Galaxia/Gutenberg, 1996 edition). Please see copyright page for full source information.

Epigraph
The book epigraph on noise and sound is quoted from an online report of the World Health Organization, *Guidelines for Community Noise*, edited by Birgitta Berglun, Thomas Lindvall, Dietrich H. Schwela, copyright WHO, 1999.

"Slippage and red poppies"
This piece is partly in response to the oil painting *Field of Poppies*, by Charles-François Daubigny (French, 1817-1878), 1874, which is in the permanent collection of the Portland Art Museum.

"Chorus as template"
This poem was written from the memory of reading a news article about a man who was not a veteran arrested for impersonating a veteran and appearing with a politician in this guise at a public event.

"Lola, America"
The words *Hey Lolly Lolly* refer to lyrics in a folk song by Woody Guthrie.

"anniversaries walking"
This poem was prompted in part from conversations with artist Linda Hutchins about simultaneity, and her process of drawing with all ten fingers simultaneously, using silver thimbles. It draws from news of the 9/11 ten-year memorial, including the oral history narrative of Keith Thomas in *The New York Times* feature *Witness to Apocalypse*, a project by researchers at the Columbia Center for Oral History, published September 8, 2011, copyright 2011 The New York Times Company. It also includes information from online birthday databases.

"Inherited travel"
The Lyn Hejinian quote which serves as an epigraph to this poem—*"Travelling is sentimental"*—is from *Zither and Autobiography*, by Leslie Scalapino. This quote is attributed by Leslie Scalapino to Lyn Hejinian. Copyright Leslie Scalapino, Wesleyan University Press, 2003.

"The tour of the abdomen of *La Verità*" and "The earphones and *La Verità*"
*La Verità* is a marble sculpture by Gian Lorenzo Bernini located in the Galleria Borghese, Rome; the sculpture was unfinished at the artist's death.

"4 rains"
The Anne Carson quote which serves as an epigraph to this poem, *"All human desire is poised on an axis of paradox, absence and presence its poles..."* is drawn from Carson's *Eros the Bittersweet*, copyright 1986 Princeton University Press, copyright 1998 Anne Carson, Dalkey Archive Press, 2009.

Endi Bogue Hartigan is author of *One Sun Storm*, which was selected for the 2008 Colorado Prize for Poetry and was a finalist for the Oregon Book Award. Her work has appeared in magazines and anthologies including *Verse, Chicago Review, Colorado Review, Pleiades, VOLT, Free Verse, Peep/Show, LVNG, Jack London is Dead,* and a collaborative chapbook, *out of the flowering ribs,* created with artist Linda Hutchins. She lives in Portland, Oregon with her husband and son.